Computer Vision with Python and OpenCV

Build Image Processing Applications with Deep Learning

Greyson Chesterfield

COPYRIGHT

DISCLAIMER

The information provided in this book is for general informational purposes only. All content in this book reflects the author's views and is based on their research, knowledge, and experiences. The author and publisher make no representations or warranties of any kind concerning the completeness, accuracy, reliability, suitability, or availability of the information contained herein.

This book is not intended to be a substitute for professional advice, diagnosis, or treatment. Readers should seek professional advice for any specific concerns or conditions. The author and publisher disclaim any liability or responsibility for any direct, indirect, incidental, or consequential loss or damage arising from the use of the information contained in this book.

Contents

What is Computer Vision?

Imagine a world where machines understand and interpret the visual world just as humans do. From unlocking your phone with your face to cars navigating busy roads without a driver, **computer vision** is at the heart of this revolution. But what exactly is computer vision?

Computer vision is a field of artificial intelligence (AI) that enables computers to analyze, process, and understand images and videos. At its core, it mimics the human ability to see, identify, and make decisions based on visual data. However, computers aren't naturally equipped to understand images; they need algorithms and models to bridge the gap between raw pixel data and meaningful insights.

Everyday Applications of Computer Vision

Computer vision has transformed numerous industries and touched everyday life in countless ways:

1. **Face Detection and Recognition**

   o Used in smartphones for unlocking devices.

   o Powers security systems in airports and offices.

   o Helps social media platforms suggest tagging friends in photos.

2. **Autonomous Vehicles**

- Self-driving cars rely on computer vision to detect lanes, pedestrians, and traffic signals.
- Cameras and sensors work in tandem to provide a real-time view of the road.

3. **Augmented Reality (AR) and Virtual Reality (VR)**

   - AR applications like Pokémon Go superimpose digital objects onto the real world.
   - VR systems provide immersive experiences by simulating environments.

4. **Medical Imaging**

   - Assists doctors in diagnosing diseases through tools like X-ray analysis and tumor detection.
   - Enables automated detection of abnormalities in CT scans and MRIs.

5. **Retail and E-Commerce**

   - Visual search tools allow customers to find products by uploading photos.
   - Inventory management systems track items in warehouses using cameras.

6. **Manufacturing and Quality Control**

   - Detects defects in products during assembly.
   - Ensures high standards of production quality in industries like electronics and automotive.

Through these applications, computer vision is improving efficiency, enhancing safety, and enriching experiences across sectors.

A Brief History of Computer Vision

The journey of computer vision began decades ago with simple experiments:

1. **1960s**: The term "computer vision" emerged as researchers explored ways for machines to interpret visual data. Early efforts focused on geometric shapes and edge detection.

2. **1970s-1980s**: Algorithms like **convolutional filters** for edge and texture detection were introduced. Computer vision remained largely academic, with limited real-world applications.

3. **1990s**: The rise of digital cameras and faster computers enabled practical experiments. Face detection algorithms gained traction, marking the first step toward mainstream adoption.

4. **2010s**: The advent of **deep learning** revolutionized computer vision. Convolutional Neural Networks (CNNs) demonstrated exceptional performance in tasks like object detection and segmentation.

Today, computer vision continues to evolve, driven by advancements in AI, hardware, and massive datasets.

Why Python and OpenCV?

Ease of Use

Python has become the de facto language for AI and computer vision due to its simplicity and versatility. Its human-readable syntax allows developers to focus on building solutions rather than wrestling with complex programming constructs.

Open-Source Community

Python boasts an extensive ecosystem of libraries and frameworks, and OpenCV (Open Source Computer Vision Library) is one of its crown jewels. OpenCV, written in C++, provides Python bindings, offering:

- Powerful tools for image and video processing.
- Support for tasks like face detection, object tracking, and feature matching.
- Community contributions, ensuring continuous improvement.

Deep Learning Integration

Python seamlessly integrates with deep learning frameworks like **TensorFlow** and **PyTorch**, which are essential for modern computer vision tasks. This combination enables developers to:

- Train custom models on datasets.
- Use pre-trained models for quick prototyping.
- Deploy solutions for real-world applications.

With Python and OpenCV, you get the best of both worlds: ease of coding and the power to build cutting-edge solutions.

Setting Up the Environment

Before diving into coding, let's ensure your development environment is ready. Here's a step-by-step guide:

1. Python Installation

Python is the backbone of your computer vision projects. Follow these steps:

- Download Python from the official website.

- Install the latest version (e.g., Python 3.10 or higher).

- Verify the installation by typing python --version in your terminal.

2. Installing Dependencies

Once Python is installed, you'll need to set up libraries for computer vision:

- **OpenCV**: Install it using pip:

bash

```
pip install opencv-python opencv-python-headless
```

- **NumPy**: Required for numerical operations:

bash

pip install numpy

- **Matplotlib** (Optional): For visualizing images and data:

bash

pip install matplotlib

For deep learning integration, consider installing:

- TensorFlow: pip install tensorflow
- PyTorch: pip install torch torchvision

3. IDE Suggestions

A robust Integrated Development Environment (IDE) can enhance your productivity:

- **Jupyter Notebook**: Ideal for experimentation and visualization. Install with:

bash

pip install notebook

- **VS Code**: A lightweight, feature-rich editor. Add the Python extension for code linting and debugging.

- **PyCharm**: Tailored for Python development, offering features like smart code completion.

Chapter 1: Basics of Image Processing

Understanding Digital Images

What is a Digital Image?

At its essence, a digital image is a numerical representation of a visual scene. It's made up of tiny units called **pixels**, which collectively form the image.

1. **Pixels**

   - A pixel is the smallest unit of a digital image.

   - Each pixel contains a numerical value that represents its intensity or color.

   - For example:

     - In a **grayscale image**, each pixel value ranges from 0 (black) to 255 (white).

     - In an **RGB image**, each pixel contains three values (Red, Green, Blue), creating a composite color.

2. **Resolution**

- o Resolution refers to the number of pixels in an image, typically represented as **width × height**.
- o Higher resolution means more detail, as the image contains more pixels.

3. **Image Channels**

- o Channels represent the layers of color information in an image:
    - ▪ **Grayscale images** have a single channel.
    - ▪ **RGB images** have three channels: Red, Green, and Blue.
- o Some images, like PNGs, may have an additional **alpha channel** for transparency.

Grayscale vs. RGB Images

1. **Grayscale Images**

- o Contain only intensity information.
- o Efficient for tasks like edge detection or thresholding.

2. **RGB Images**

- o Contain three channels, allowing for full-color representation.
- o Used for applications where color details are crucial (e.g., object detection).

Example: Think of a grayscale image as a pencil sketch, while an RGB image is like a vibrant painting.

Core OpenCV Functions

OpenCV simplifies working with digital images, offering a robust toolkit for manipulation and analysis. Let's explore some fundamental functions.

Reading, Displaying, and Saving Images

1. **Reading an Image**

   o   Use cv2.imread() to load an image.

   o   Example:

python

```
import cv2

image = cv2.imread('example.jpg')  # Reads the image in
color by default
```

2. **Displaying an Image**

   o   Use cv2.imshow() to display an image in a window.

   o   Example:

python

cv2.imshow('Image Window', image)

cv2.waitKey(0) # Wait until a key is pressed

cv2.destroyAllWindows() # Close the window

3. **Saving an Image**

   o   Use cv2.imwrite() to save an image.

   o   Example:

python

cv2.imwrite('output.jpg', image)

Basic Manipulations

1. **Resizing an Image**

   o   Adjust the dimensions of an image using cv2.resize().

   o   Example:

python

resized_image = cv2.resize(image, (200, 300)) # Resizes to 200x300 pixels

2. **Cropping an Image**

   o   Extract a portion of the image using slicing.

o Example:

python

cropped_image = image[50:200, 100:300] # Crop from (50,100) to (200,300)

3. **Rotating an Image**

o Rotate an image using cv2.getRotationMatrix2D() and cv2.warpAffine().

o Example:

python

rows, cols = image.shape[:2]

matrix = cv2.getRotationMatrix2D((cols/2, rows/2), 90, 1) # 90 degrees

rotated_image = cv2.warpAffine(image, matrix, (cols, rows))

4. **Flipping an Image**

o Flip vertically, horizontally, or both using cv2.flip().

o Example:

python

flipped_image = cv2.flip(image, 1) # Horizontal flip

Hands-On: Image Transformations

Applying Transformations in a Workflow

Let's perform a series of transformations on an image step-by-step to reinforce your understanding.

1. **Read the Image**

python

```
image = cv2.imread('example.jpg')
```

2. **Convert to Grayscale**

   ○ Example:

python

```
gray_image = cv2.cvtColor(image,
cv2.COLOR_BGR2GRAY)

cv2.imshow('Grayscale Image', gray_image)

cv2.waitKey(0)

cv2.destroyAllWindows()
```

3. **Resize the Image**

   ○ Reduce the image size for faster processing.

python

```python
resized_image = cv2.resize(image, (100, 100))  # Resize to 100x100
```

4. **Crop a Region of Interest (ROI)**
   - Example:

python

```python
roi = image[50:150, 50:150]
```

5. **Apply a Flip**
   - Flip horizontally.

python

```python
flipped_image = cv2.flip(image, 1)
```

6. **Save the Transformed Image**
   - Save the flipped image.

python

```python
cv2.imwrite('flipped_output.jpg', flipped_image)
```

End-to-End Mini-Project

Goal: Create a grayscale thumbnail of an image.

Steps:

1. Load the image.

2. Convert it to grayscale.

3. Resize it to a thumbnail size (e.g., 50x50 pixels).

4. Save the final image.

Code:

python

```python
import cv2

# Step 1: Read the image
image = cv2.imread('example.jpg')

# Step 2: Convert to grayscale
gray_image = cv2.cvtColor(image,
cv2.COLOR_BGR2GRAY)

# Step 3: Resize to a thumbnail
thumbnail = cv2.resize(gray_image, (50, 50))

# Step 4: Save the thumbnail
cv2.imwrite('thumbnail.jpg', thumbnail)

print("Thumbnail created and saved as thumbnail.jpg")
```

Chapter 2: Working with Video Streams

Capturing Video with OpenCV

Video processing is an essential aspect of computer vision, allowing us to analyze and manipulate motion and time-based visual data. OpenCV provides robust tools for capturing and handling video streams, whether from webcams or video files.

Webcam Input

Capturing a live video feed from a webcam is straightforward with OpenCV. The core function for video capture is cv2.VideoCapture().

1. **Basic Webcam Capture**

    o   Example:

```python
import cv2


# Open the default webcam (use 0 for the first camera)
```

```python
cap = cv2.VideoCapture(0)

while True:
    ret, frame = cap.read()  # Read a frame from the webcam
    if not ret:
        print("Failed to grab frame.")
        break

    cv2.imshow("Webcam Feed", frame)  # Display the frame

    # Exit loop on pressing 'q'
    if cv2.waitKey(1) & 0xFF == ord('q'):
        break

cap.release()  # Release the camera resource
cv2.destroyAllWindows()
```

2. **Customizing Webcam Settings**
   - You can adjust properties like frame width, height, and brightness:

python

```python
cap.set(cv2.CAP_PROP_FRAME_WIDTH, 640)  # Set width
```

```python
cap.set(cv2.CAP_PROP_FRAME_HEIGHT, 480)  # Set height
```

Video File Processing

OpenCV allows you to load and process video files in the same way as webcam feeds, but with the additional ability to navigate through frames.

1. **Reading a Video File**

   o   Example:

python

```python
cap = cv2.VideoCapture('input_video.mp4')  # Load a video file
```

```python
while cap.isOpened():
    ret, frame = cap.read()
    if not ret:
        print("Video ended.")
        break

    cv2.imshow("Video Playback", frame)
```

```
# Exit loop on pressing 'q'

if cv2.waitKey(25) & 0xFF == ord('q'):

    break


cap.release()

cv2.destroyAllWindows()
```

2. **Extracting Video Properties**

   o Example:

python

```
fps = cap.get(cv2.CAP_PROP_FPS)  # Frames per second

width = int(cap.get(cv2.CAP_PROP_FRAME_WIDTH))

height = int(cap.get(cv2.CAP_PROP_FRAME_HEIGHT))


print(f"Video Properties - FPS: {fps}, Width: {width}, Height: {height}")
```

Real-World Example: Building a Motion Detector

A motion detector identifies changes in a video feed by comparing successive frames. This technique has applications in surveillance, security, and automated systems.

Steps to Build a Motion Detector

1. Capture video from a webcam or video file.

2. Convert frames to grayscale to simplify processing.

3. Compute the difference between consecutive frames.

4. Threshold the difference to highlight moving objects.

5. Display the results.

Code Implementation

python

```
import cv2
import numpy as np


# Initialize video capture
cap = cv2.VideoCapture(0)  # Use webcam (or replace with a video file path)


# Initialize a background frame
_, first_frame = cap.read()
first_frame_gray = cv2.cvtColor(first_frame, cv2.COLOR_BGR2GRAY)
```

```python
    first_frame_gray = cv2.GaussianBlur(first_frame_gray,
    (21, 21), 0)


    while cap.isOpened():
        ret, frame = cap.read()
        if not ret:
            break


        # Convert the current frame to grayscale and blur it
        gray_frame = cv2.cvtColor(frame,
    cv2.COLOR_BGR2GRAY)
        gray_frame = cv2.GaussianBlur(gray_frame, (21, 21), 0)


        # Compute the absolute difference between the first
    frame and current frame
        frame_diff = cv2.absdiff(first_frame_gray, gray_frame)


        # Apply a binary threshold to the difference
        _, threshold_frame = cv2.threshold(frame_diff, 25, 255,
    cv2.THRESH_BINARY)


        # Dilate the thresholded image to fill gaps
        threshold_frame = cv2.dilate(threshold_frame, None,
    iterations=2)
```

```
# Display the motion areas
cv2.imshow("Motion Detection", threshold_frame)
cv2.imshow("Original Video", frame)

# Exit loop on pressing 'q'
if cv2.waitKey(10) & 0xFF == ord('q'):
    break

cap.release()
cv2.destroyAllWindows()
```

Explanation

- **Blurring**: Smoothens images to reduce noise.
- **Frame Difference**: Highlights areas of movement.
- **Thresholding**: Converts the difference into a binary image for clarity.

Video Manipulations

Frame Extraction

Frames are the individual images that make up a video. Extracting frames allows us to process videos frame by frame.

1. **Extract Frames from a Video File**

    o Example:

python

```
cap = cv2.VideoCapture('input_video.mp4')
frame_count = 0

while cap.isOpened():
    ret, frame = cap.read()
    if not ret:
        break

    # Save each frame as an image file
    cv2.imwrite(f'frame_{frame_count:04d}.jpg', frame)
    frame_count += 1

cap.release()
```

Frame Rate Adjustments

Frame rate determines the speed of playback. Adjusting it can speed up or slow down the video.

1. **Change Playback Speed**

    o Example:

```python
cap = cv2.VideoCapture('input_video.mp4')
delay = int(1000 / cap.get(cv2.CAP_PROP_FPS))  # Calculate delay for normal playback

while cap.isOpened():
    ret, frame = cap.read()
    if not ret:
        break

    cv2.imshow("Video Playback", frame)
    if cv2.waitKey(delay) & 0xFF == ord('q'):  # Adjust delay for faster/slower playback
        break

cap.release()
cv2.destroyAllWindows()
```

Chapter 3: Image Enhancement Techniques

Image enhancement improves the quality of images, making them clearer, more interpretable, and ready for further analysis. This chapter covers key techniques in filtering, edge detection, and contrast adjustment, illustrated through practical applications.

Image Filtering

Image filtering involves transforming the pixel values of an image to emphasize or reduce certain features. OpenCV provides robust tools for filtering images to achieve effects like smoothing, sharpening, and edge detection.

1. Smoothing

Smoothing reduces noise in an image, making it visually appealing and suitable for applications like feature detection.

- **Averaging Filter**: Computes the average of pixel values in a neighborhood.
    - o Code:

python

```python
import cv2
import numpy as np

image = cv2.imread('example.jpg')
smoothed = cv2.blur(image, (5, 5))  # 5x5 kernel
cv2.imshow('Smoothed Image', smoothed)
cv2.waitKey(0)
cv2.destroyAllWindows()
```

- **Gaussian Blur**: Weights neighboring pixels with a Gaussian distribution, reducing noise while preserving edges.

    o Code:

python

```python
blurred = cv2.GaussianBlur(image, (5, 5), 0)  # Standard deviation = 0
```

- **Median Filtering**: Replaces each pixel with the median value in its neighborhood, excellent for reducing salt-and-pepper noise.

    o Code:

python

```python
median = cv2.medianBlur(image, 5)
```

---

2. Sharpening

Sharpening enhances edges and fine details in an image.

- **Laplacian Filter**: Highlights edges by calculating the second derivative of pixel intensities.

  o Code:

python

```python
laplacian = cv2.Laplacian(image, cv2.CV_64F)
laplacian = cv2.convertScaleAbs(laplacian)  # Convert back to 8-bit
cv2.imshow('Sharpened Image', laplacian)
cv2.waitKey(0)
cv2.destroyAllWindows()
```

- **Custom Kernel for Sharpening**:

  o Example:

python

```python
kernel = np.array([[0, -1, 0],
                   [-1, 5, -1],
                   [0, -1, 0]])
sharpened = cv2.filter2D(image, -1, kernel)
```

3. Edge Detection

Edge detection highlights the boundaries of objects in an image.

- **Canny Edge Detection**:

  - Steps: Apply Gaussian blur → Compute gradients → Apply thresholding.

  - Code:

python

```
edges = cv2.Canny(image, 100, 200)  # Low and high thresholds

cv2.imshow('Edges', edges)

cv2.waitKey(0)
```

Real-World Example: Building a Document Scanner

Let's use these techniques to create a document scanner. The goal is to detect the document in an image, apply perspective transformation, and enhance its readability.

Steps to Build a Document Scanner:

1. Read the input image.

2. Convert it to grayscale and apply edge detection.

3. Find the largest contour (the document boundary).

4. Perform a perspective transformation to extract the document.

5. Apply sharpening to enhance text readability.

Code Implementation:

python

```python
import cv2
import numpy as np


# Step 1: Load the image
image = cv2.imread('document.jpg')
original = image.copy()


# Step 2: Convert to grayscale
gray = cv2.cvtColor(image, cv2.COLOR_BGR2GRAY)


# Step 3: Apply Gaussian Blur and Edge Detection
blurred = cv2.GaussianBlur(gray, (5, 5), 0)
edges = cv2.Canny(blurred, 50, 150)


# Step 4: Find contours
```

```python
contours, _ = cv2.findContours(edges,
cv2.RETR_EXTERNAL,
cv2.CHAIN_APPROX_SIMPLE)

contours = sorted(contours, key=cv2.contourArea,
reverse=True)


# Step 5: Get the largest contour

for contour in contours:

    perimeter = cv2.arcLength(contour, True)

    approx = cv2.approxPolyDP(contour, 0.02 * perimeter,
True)


    if len(approx) == 4:  # Document should have 4 corners

        document_contour = approx

        break


# Step 6: Perform perspective transformation

pts = document_contour.reshape(4, 2)

rect = np.zeros((4, 2), dtype="float32")


# Order points: top-left, top-right, bottom-right, bottom-left

s = pts.sum(axis=1)

rect[0] = pts[np.argmin(s)]
```

```python
rect[2] = pts[np.argmax(s)]

diff = np.diff(pts, axis=1)
rect[1] = pts[np.argmin(diff)]
rect[3] = pts[np.argmax(diff)]

(width, height) = (500, 700)  # Desired output size
dst = np.array([
    [0, 0],
    [width - 1, 0],
    [width - 1, height - 1],
    [0, height - 1]], dtype="float32")

M = cv2.getPerspectiveTransform(rect, dst)
warped = cv2.warpPerspective(original, M, (width, height))

# Step 7: Sharpen the scanned document
kernel = np.array([[0, -1, 0],
                   [-1, 5, -1],
                   [0, -1, 0]])
sharpened = cv2.filter2D(warped, -1, kernel)
```

```python
cv2.imshow('Scanned Document', sharpened)
cv2.waitKey(0)
cv2.destroyAllWindows()
```

Histogram Equalization

Histogram equalization enhances image contrast by redistributing pixel intensities. It is particularly effective for low-light images.

How It Works

- The intensity histogram of an image shows the distribution of pixel values.

- Histogram equalization spreads the pixel values more uniformly, improving visibility.

Steps in OpenCV

1. **Grayscale Histogram Equalization:**

   o Code:

python

```python
gray = cv2.cvtColor(image, cv2.COLOR_BGR2GRAY)
equalized = cv2.equalizeHist(gray)
```

```
cv2.imshow('Original', gray)

cv2.imshow('Equalized', equalized)

cv2.waitKey(0)
```

2. Color Histogram Equalization:

- o Apply histogram equalization to each channel separately in the HSV color space.

- o Code:

python

```
hsv = cv2.cvtColor(image, cv2.COLOR_BGR2HSV)

hsv[:, :, 2] = cv2.equalizeHist(hsv[:, :, 2])  # Apply to Value channel

equalized_image = cv2.cvtColor(hsv, cv2.COLOR_HSV2BGR)
```

Real-World Application

Improving the visibility of an underexposed image, such as a nighttime photo or poorly lit document, is a common use case.

Example Workflow:

1. Convert the image to grayscale.

2. Apply histogram equalization.

3. Save the enhanced result.

Chapter 4: Object Detection and Tracking

Object detection and tracking are essential in computer vision for identifying and monitoring objects in images or video streams. This chapter introduces contour-based object detection and filtering techniques, followed by real-world applications and tracking algorithms like MeanShift and CamShift.

Contours and Shape Detection

Contours are curves joining continuous points along a boundary that share the same intensity. OpenCV provides robust tools for detecting and analyzing contours to identify objects in an image.

Detecting Objects Using Contours

Contours are extracted using edge detection or thresholding, followed by the cv2.findContours() function.

1. **Steps to Detect Contours**:

   o Convert the image to grayscale.

- Apply thresholding or edge detection to highlight object boundaries.
- Use cv2.findContours() to extract contours.

2. **Code Example**:

python

```python
import cv2

# Load the image
image = cv2.imread('shapes.jpg')
gray = cv2.cvtColor(image, cv2.COLOR_BGR2GRAY)

# Apply thresholding
_, thresholded = cv2.threshold(gray, 127, 255, cv2.THRESH_BINARY)

# Find contours
contours, _ = cv2.findContours(thresholded, cv2.RETR_EXTERNAL, cv2.CHAIN_APPROX_SIMPLE)

# Draw contours
cv2.drawContours(image, contours, -1, (0, 255, 0), 2)  # Draw all contours
```

```
cv2.imshow('Contours', image)

cv2.waitKey(0)

cv2.destroyAllWindows()
```

Filtering by Area, Shape, and Orientation

1. **Filtering by Area**:
   - Eliminate noise by considering only contours within a specific size range.
   - Example:

python

```
for contour in contours:
    area = cv2.contourArea(contour)
    if area > 100:  # Filter small objects
        cv2.drawContours(image, [contour], -1, (255, 0, 0), 2)
```

2. **Approximating Contour Shapes**:
   - Approximate a contour to a simpler polygon using cv2.approxPolyDP().
   - Example:

python

```
for contour in contours:

    perimeter = cv2.arcLength(contour, True)

    approx = cv2.approxPolyDP(contour, 0.02 * perimeter,
True)

    if len(approx) == 3:  # Triangle

        cv2.drawContours(image, [contour], -1, (0, 255, 0), 2)
```

3. **Orientation Detection**:

   o Determine the angle of objects using
      cv2.minAreaRect().

   o Example:

python

```
for contour in contours:

    rect = cv2.minAreaRect(contour)

    angle = rect[-1]  # Angle of the bounding box

    print(f"Object Angle: {angle}")
```

Real-World Example: Counting Objects in an Image

Task: Count coins in an image by detecting their contours and filtering based on size.

Steps:

1. Load the image and preprocess it (grayscale and threshold).

2. Find contours and filter based on area.

3. Count the filtered contours.

Code:

python

```
import cv2


# Load the image
image = cv2.imread('coins.jpg')
gray = cv2.cvtColor(image, cv2.COLOR_BGR2GRAY)


# Apply Gaussian blur and thresholding
blurred = cv2.GaussianBlur(gray, (5, 5), 0)
_, thresholded = cv2.threshold(blurred, 100, 255,
cv2.THRESH_BINARY)


# Find contours
contours, _ = cv2.findContours(thresholded,
cv2.RETR_EXTERNAL,
cv2.CHAIN_APPROX_SIMPLE)
```

```python
# Filter and count coins

coin_count = 0

for contour in contours:

    area = cv2.contourArea(contour)

    if 1000 < area < 5000:  # Assume coin size falls in this range

        coin_count += 1

        cv2.drawContours(image, [contour], -1, (0, 255, 0), 2)


print(f"Total Coins Detected: {coin_count}")


cv2.imshow('Detected Coins', image)

cv2.waitKey(0)

cv2.destroyAllWindows()
```

Tracking Algorithms

Tracking involves following objects across frames in a video. Two popular algorithms in OpenCV are **MeanShift** and **CamShift**.

MeanShift

MeanShift is a clustering-based tracking algorithm that iteratively shifts the region of interest toward the densest part of the feature space.

1. **Steps**:

   o Define an initial region of interest (ROI).

   o Compute a histogram of the ROI.

   o Update the ROI location to maximize similarity in the next frame.

2. **Code Example**:

python

```python
import cv2


# Load the video
cap = cv2.VideoCapture('video.mp4')


# Define the initial ROI
ret, frame = cap.read()
roi = cv2.selectROI("Select ROI", frame, fromCenter=False, showCrosshair=True)
x, y, w, h = int(roi[0]), int(roi[1]), int(roi[2]), int(roi[3])


# Create a histogram of the ROI
```

```python
roi_frame = frame[y:y+h, x:x+w]

hsv_roi = cv2.cvtColor(roi_frame,
cv2.COLOR_BGR2HSV)

roi_hist = cv2.calcHist([hsv_roi], [0], None, [180], [0,
180])

cv2.normalize(roi_hist, roi_hist, 0, 255,
cv2.NORM_MINMAX)


# Termination criteria: 10 iterations or move by at least 1
pixel

term_crit = (cv2.TERM_CRITERIA_EPS |
cv2.TERM_CRITERIA_COUNT, 10, 1)


while True:
    ret, frame = cap.read()
    if not ret:
        break


    hsv = cv2.cvtColor(frame, cv2.COLOR_BGR2HSV)
    back_proj = cv2.calcBackProject([hsv], [0], roi_hist, [0,
180], 1)


    # Apply MeanShift
```

```
    ret, roi = cv2.meanShift(back_proj, (x, y, w, h),
term_crit)

    x, y, w, h = roi


    # Draw the updated ROI

    cv2.rectangle(frame, (x, y), (x + w, y + h), (0, 255, 0), 2)

    cv2.imshow('MeanShift Tracking', frame)


    if cv2.waitKey(30) & 0xFF == ord('q'):

        break


cap.release()

cv2.destroyAllWindows()
```

CamShift

CamShift (Continuously Adaptive MeanShift) extends MeanShift by adjusting the size of the tracking window dynamically.

1. **Differences from MeanShift**:
   - Adjusts the size of the ROI based on the object's scale.
   - Outputs the rotated bounding box.

2. **Code Example**:

python

```
import cv2

# Load the video
cap = cv2.VideoCapture('video.mp4')

# Define the initial ROI
ret, frame = cap.read()
roi = cv2.selectROI("Select ROI", frame,
fromCenter=False, showCrosshair=True)
x, y, w, h = int(roi[0]), int(roi[1]), int(roi[2]), int(roi[3])

# Create a histogram of the ROI
roi_frame = frame[y:y+h, x:x+w]
hsv_roi = cv2.cvtColor(roi_frame,
cv2.COLOR_BGR2HSV)
roi_hist = cv2.calcHist([hsv_roi], [0], None, [180], [0,
180])
cv2.normalize(roi_hist, roi_hist, 0, 255,
cv2.NORM_MINMAX)
```

```python
# Termination criteria
term_crit = (cv2.TERM_CRITERIA_EPS |
cv2.TERM_CRITERIA_COUNT, 10, 1)

while True:
    ret, frame = cap.read()
    if not ret:
        break

    hsv = cv2.cvtColor(frame, cv2.COLOR_BGR2HSV)
    back_proj = cv2.calcBackProject([hsv], [0], roi_hist, [0,
180], 1)

    # Apply CamShift
    ret, track_window = cv2.CamShift(back_proj, (x, y, w,
h), term_crit)
    x, y, w, h = track_window

    # Draw the tracking box
    pts = cv2.boxPoints(ret)
    pts = np.int0(pts)
    cv2.polylines(frame, [pts], True, (0, 255, 0), 2)
    cv2.imshow('CamShift Tracking', frame)
```

```python
    if cv2.waitKey(30) & 0xFF == ord('q'):
        break

cap.release()
cv2.destroyAllWindows()
```

Chapter 5: Machine Learning with OpenCV

Machine learning empowers computer vision by enabling systems to learn from data and make intelligent predictions. While deep learning dominates many computer vision tasks today, classical machine learning models like **K-Nearest Neighbors (KNN)**, **Support Vector Machines (SVM)**, and **K-Means Clustering** remain powerful tools for simpler and smaller-scale problems.

In this chapter, we'll explore these classical models and their applications, culminating in a practical example of handwritten digit recognition using SVM.

Introduction to Classical Models

1. K-Nearest Neighbors (KNN)

KNN is one of the simplest supervised learning algorithms. It classifies data points based on the majority class of their **k nearest neighbors**.

1. **How It Works**:

    o   The algorithm computes the distance between a query point and all training points.

- o It identifies the k nearest points and assigns the class most common among them.

2. **Strengths**:

   - o Simple to implement.

   - o Effective for smaller datasets.

3. **Weaknesses**:

   - o Computationally expensive for large datasets.

   - o Sensitive to irrelevant features and noisy data.

---

2. Support Vector Machines (SVM)

SVM is a supervised learning algorithm used for classification and regression. It works by finding the **hyperplane** that best separates data points of different classes.

1. **Key Concepts**:

   - o **Hyperplane**: A decision boundary between classes.

   - o **Margin**: The distance between the hyperplane and the nearest data points of each class. SVM maximizes this margin.

   - o **Kernel Trick**: Transforms non-linearly separable data into a higher dimension for better separation.

2. **Applications**:

- o Text classification.
- o Image recognition (e.g., handwritten digit classification).

---

3. K-Means Clustering

K-Means is an unsupervised learning algorithm used for clustering data into k groups.

1. **How It Works**:
   - o Randomly initialize k cluster centroids.
   - o Assign each point to the nearest centroid.
   - o Update centroids by averaging the points in each cluster.
   - o Repeat until convergence.

2. **Applications**:
   - o Color quantization in images.
   - o Grouping similar objects.

Practical Example: Handwritten Digit Recognition Using SVM

Objective

Classify handwritten digits (0-9) using the SVM model in OpenCV with the popular **MNIST** dataset or similar.

Dataset

MNIST is a dataset of 28x28 grayscale images of digits. Each digit is labeled from 0 to 9.

Steps to Build the Model

1. Load and Preprocess the Data

- o Flatten the 28x28 images into 1D arrays (784 features).

- o Normalize pixel values to a range of 0 to 1 for consistent input.

2. Train the SVM Model

- o Split the dataset into training and testing sets.

- o Use OpenCV's cv2.ml.SVM_create() to define the model.

- o Train the SVM using the training data.

3. Evaluate the Model

- o Test the model on unseen data.

- o Compute accuracy and visualize predictions.

Code Implementation

python

```python
import cv2
import numpy as np
from sklearn.model_selection import train_test_split
from sklearn.datasets import fetch_openml


# Step 1: Load the MNIST Dataset
print("Loading MNIST dataset...")
mnist = fetch_openml('mnist_784', version=1)
data = mnist.data / 255.0  # Normalize pixel values to [0, 1]
labels = mnist.target.astype(np.int32)  # Convert labels to
integers


# Step 2: Split the data into training and testing sets
X_train, X_test, y_train, y_test = train_test_split(data,
labels, test_size=0.2, random_state=42)


# Step 3: Define and Train the SVM Model
print("Training the SVM model...")
svm = cv2.ml.SVM_create()
svm.setKernel(cv2.ml.SVM_RBF)  # Use Radial Basis
Function kernel
svm.setType(cv2.ml.SVM_C_SVC)  # C-Support Vector
Classification
```

```python
svm.setC(2.5)  # Regularization parameter
svm.setGamma(0.05)  # Kernel coefficient


# Train the model
svm.train(X_train.astype(np.float32),
cv2.ml.ROW_SAMPLE, y_train)


# Step 4: Test the Model
print("Testing the SVM model...")
_, predictions = svm.predict(X_test.astype(np.float32))
accuracy = np.mean(predictions == y_test)


print(f"Model Accuracy: {accuracy * 100:.2f}%")


# Step 5: Visualize Predictions
def display_sample(index):
    """Displays an image and its prediction."""
    img = X_test[index].reshape(28, 28)
    cv2.imshow(f"Prediction: {int(predictions[index])}",
img)
    cv2.waitKey(0)
    cv2.destroyAllWindows()
```

display_sample(0) # Display the first test image and its prediction

---

Explanation

1. **Data Loading and Normalization**:

   o   MNIST is normalized to ensure consistent input to the SVM.

2. **Kernel Choice**:

   o   RBF kernel is chosen for its ability to handle non-linear data.

3. **Evaluation**:

   o   Accuracy is computed as the ratio of correct predictions to total samples.

   o   Visualizing test samples helps verify predictions.

Discussion

- SVM performs well for smaller datasets like MNIST but may struggle with large-scale problems.

- Consider deep learning (e.g., Convolutional Neural Networks) for more complex datasets.

Extensions: Enhancing Handwritten Digit Recognition

Improving Performance

- **Feature Engineering**: Use image features like edges and contours.

- **Hyperparameter Tuning**: Optimize C and gamma for better classification.

Applications

- Digit recognition is foundational for OCR (Optical Character Recognition) systems, which are widely used in:

    o Postal address reading.

    o Bank check digitization.

    o Form automation.

Chapter 6: Deep Learning Foundations

Deep learning has revolutionized computer vision by enabling machines to achieve human-level understanding of images and videos. This chapter explores the need for deep learning in computer vision, introduces Convolutional Neural Networks (CNNs), and provides an overview of tools like TensorFlow, Keras, and PyTorch.

Why Deep Learning in Computer Vision?

Traditional computer vision methods rely heavily on handcrafted features and algorithms to extract information from images. While these methods work well for specific tasks, they fall short in scalability and adaptability.

Advantages of Deep Learning

1. **Automatic Feature Extraction**:

- o Deep learning models learn features directly from raw data.

- o This eliminates the need for manual engineering of features like edges or textures.

2. **Handling Complexity**:

   - o Traditional methods struggle with complex tasks such as object recognition in diverse environments.

   - o Deep learning excels in understanding intricate patterns and variations.

3. **Scalability**:

   - o Neural networks can process large datasets and improve with more data.

   - o Traditional algorithms often plateau in performance with increasing data size.

4. **End-to-End Learning**:

   - o Deep learning models process raw input data and output predictions in one pipeline.

   - o This makes them efficient for tasks like image classification, segmentation, and detection.

5. **Transfer Learning**:

   - o Pre-trained deep learning models like ResNet or MobileNet can be fine-tuned for specific tasks, saving time and computational resources.

Introduction to Convolutional Neural Networks (CNNs)

Convolutional Neural Networks (CNNs) are the cornerstone of modern computer vision. They mimic the way humans process visual data by identifying hierarchical patterns like edges, shapes, and objects.

Key Components of CNNs

1. **Convolutional Layers**:

    o The convolution operation applies a filter (kernel) to the input image to extract features.

    o For example, an edge-detection kernel highlights edges in an image.

    o Formula:

$$(I*K)(x,y)=\sum_m\sum_n I(m,n)\cdot K(x-m,y-n)(I * K)(x, y) = \sum_m \sum_n I(m, n) \cdot K(x-m, y-n)(I*K)(x,y)=m\sum n\sum I(m,n)\cdot K(x-m,y-n)$$

    o Code Example:

python

```
from keras.models import Sequential

from keras.layers import Conv2D
```

```python
model = Sequential([

    Conv2D(filters=32, kernel_size=(3, 3), activation='relu',
    input_shape=(28, 28, 1))

])
```

2. **Feature Maps**:
   - Output of the convolution layer, representing the activation of a filter across the input image.

3. **Pooling Layers**:
   - Pooling reduces the spatial dimensions of feature maps, making the network more efficient.
   - Common pooling techniques:
     - **Max Pooling**: Selects the maximum value in each region.
     - **Average Pooling**: Computes the average value in each region.
   - Code Example:

python

```python
from keras.layers import MaxPooling2D

model.add(MaxPooling2D(pool_size=(2, 2)))
```

4. **Fully Connected Layers**:

   o Flatten the feature maps and pass them to dense layers for final classification.

   o Code Example:

python

```
from keras.layers import Flatten, Dense

model.add(Flatten())
model.add(Dense(units=128, activation='relu'))
model.add(Dense(units=10, activation='softmax'))
```

How CNNs Work

1. Input Image:

   o An image (e.g., 28x28 pixels for grayscale, 28x28x3 for RGB) is fed into the network.

2. Feature Extraction:

   o Convolution and pooling layers extract hierarchical features.

3. Classification:

- o Fully connected layers combine features to classify the image into categories.

CNN Architecture Example

A simple CNN for classifying handwritten digits (MNIST dataset):

1. **Input**: 28x28 grayscale images.

2. **Convolution + Pooling**: Extract features.

3. **Fully Connected Layers**: Perform classification.

Code:

python

```python
from keras.models import Sequential
from keras.layers import Conv2D, MaxPooling2D, Flatten, Dense

# Define the CNN
model = Sequential([
    Conv2D(filters=32, kernel_size=(3, 3), activation='relu', input_shape=(28, 28, 1)),
    MaxPooling2D(pool_size=(2, 2)),
    Flatten(),
    Dense(units=128, activation='relu'),
```

```
    Dense(units=10, activation='softmax')
])


# Compile the model
model.compile(optimizer='adam',
loss='categorical_crossentropy', metrics=['accuracy'])


# Train the model (example data required)
# model.fit(X_train, y_train, epochs=5,
validation_data=(X_test, y_test))
```

Tools Overview

Implementing deep learning models requires powerful frameworks. TensorFlow, Keras, and PyTorch are the most popular tools in the field.

---

1. TensorFlow

TensorFlow is an open-source deep learning framework developed by Google. It provides flexibility for building complex architectures.

- **Key Features**:
  - Comprehensive for both research and production.

- o Supports GPU acceleration for faster computations.

- **Code Example**: Building a simple neural network.

python

```python
import tensorflow as tf

model = tf.keras.Sequential([
    tf.keras.layers.Dense(128, activation='relu', input_shape=(784,)),
    tf.keras.layers.Dense(10, activation='softmax')
])

model.compile(optimizer='adam', loss='categorical_crossentropy', metrics=['accuracy'])
```

---

2. Keras

Keras is a high-level API built on top of TensorFlow, designed for rapid prototyping and ease of use.

- **Key Features**:
  - o Simple and user-friendly.
  - o Allows switching between backends like TensorFlow or Theano.
- **Code Example**: Using Keras to build a CNN.

python

```python
from keras.models import Sequential
from keras.layers import Conv2D, MaxPooling2D, Flatten, Dense

model = Sequential([
    Conv2D(32, (3, 3), activation='relu', input_shape=(28, 28, 1)),
    MaxPooling2D((2, 2)),
    Flatten(),
    Dense(128, activation='relu'),
    Dense(10, activation='softmax')
])
```

---

3. PyTorch

PyTorch, developed by Facebook, is a popular choice for dynamic computation graphs and research-level projects.

- **Key Features**:
  - Dynamic graphing allows changes to the network during runtime.
  - Strong community support and integration with research tools.
- **Code Example**: Building a simple neural network.

```python
import torch
import torch.nn as nn

class NeuralNet(nn.Module):
    def __init__(self):
        super(NeuralNet, self).__init__()
        self.fc1 = nn.Linear(784, 128)
        self.fc2 = nn.Linear(128, 10)

    def forward(self, x):
        x = torch.relu(self.fc1(x))
        x = torch.softmax(self.fc2(x), dim=1)
        return x

model = NeuralNet()
```

Which Tool to Choose?

- **TensorFlow**: Best for large-scale projects and production pipelines.
- **Keras**: Ideal for beginners and quick prototyping.

- **PyTorch**: Preferred for research and dynamic experimentation.

Chapter 7: Building Deep Learning Models

In this chapter, you'll learn how to build deep learning models for image classification. We'll explore two approaches: leveraging pre-trained models via **transfer learning** and constructing a **custom CNN**. By the end, you'll gain hands-on experience with both methods.

Using Pre-Trained Models

Pre-trained models are deep learning models trained on large datasets, such as ImageNet, with millions of images. They serve as a foundation for transfer learning, where we adapt the pre-trained models to new tasks, saving time and computational resources.

Transfer Learning with MobileNet and ResNet

1. **What is Transfer Learning?**

   - Transfer learning involves fine-tuning a pre-trained model on a smaller dataset.

   - For example, a model trained to classify 1,000 ImageNet categories can be adapted to classify cats and dogs.

2. **Why Use Pre-Trained Models?**

   - **Faster Training**: Only a few layers need retraining.

   - **Reduced Data Requirements**: Leverages knowledge from large datasets.

   - **High Accuracy**: Pre-trained weights provide a solid starting point.

MobileNet

- MobileNet is a lightweight model designed for mobile and embedded devices.

- It uses depthwise separable convolutions to reduce computational cost.

ResNet (Residual Networks)

- ResNet introduces **residual connections**, which solve the vanishing gradient problem in deep networks.

- ResNet models like ResNet-50 are widely used for their accuracy and efficiency.

Hands-On: Fine-Tuning with Transfer Learning

Let's fine-tune a pre-trained MobileNet model to classify flowers using a custom dataset.

Steps:

1. Load the pre-trained model.
2. Replace the final layers with custom layers for the new task.
3. Freeze earlier layers to retain pre-trained weights.
4. Train the model on the custom dataset.

Code:

python

```python
import tensorflow as tf
from tensorflow.keras.applications import MobileNetV2
from tensorflow.keras.models import Model
from tensorflow.keras.layers import Dense, Flatten, Dropout
from tensorflow.keras.preprocessing.image import ImageDataGenerator


# Step 1: Load Pre-trained MobileNet
base_model = MobileNetV2(weights='imagenet', include_top=False, input_shape=(224, 224, 3))


# Step 2: Add Custom Layers
x = Flatten()(base_model.output)
x = Dense(128, activation='relu')(x)
```

```python
x = Dropout(0.5)(x)

output_layer = Dense(5, activation='softmax')(x)  #
Assuming 5 flower categories


model = Model(inputs=base_model.input,
outputs=output_layer)


# Step 3: Freeze Base Layers
for layer in base_model.layers:
    layer.trainable = False


# Step 4: Compile the Model
model.compile(optimizer='adam',
loss='categorical_crossentropy', metrics=['accuracy'])


# Step 5: Load and Preprocess Data
datagen = ImageDataGenerator(rescale=1./255,
validation_split=0.2)


train_generator = datagen.flow_from_directory(
    'flowers',  # Directory containing flower images
    target_size=(224, 224),
    batch_size=32,
```

```python
    class_mode='categorical',
    subset='training'
)

validation_generator = datagen.flow_from_directory(
    'flowers',
    target_size=(224, 224),
    batch_size=32,
    class_mode='categorical',
    subset='validation'
)

# Step 6: Train the Model
model.fit(
    train_generator,
    validation_data=validation_generator,
    epochs=10
)

# Step 7: Evaluate the Model
loss, accuracy = model.evaluate(validation_generator)
print(f"Validation Accuracy: {accuracy * 100:.2f}%")
```

Building a Custom CNN

For simpler tasks or educational purposes, building a CNN from scratch offers greater control and insight into its inner workings.

Example Project: Classifying Images of Dogs vs. Cats

Dataset

- Use a dataset like Kaggle's Cats vs. Dogs dataset.
- Each image belongs to one of two categories: dog or cat.

Steps to Build a Custom CNN

1. **Load and Preprocess the Dataset**
   o Resize images to a fixed size.
   o Normalize pixel values to a range of 0 to 1.

2. **Define the CNN Architecture**
   o Convolutional layers for feature extraction.
   o Pooling layers for spatial reduction.
   o Fully connected layers for classification.

3. **Compile and Train the Model**

- Use appropriate loss functions (e.g., binary crossentropy) and optimizers (e.g., Adam).

4. **Evaluate and Test**

   - Measure accuracy and visualize predictions.

Code Implementation

python

```
import tensorflow as tf

from tensorflow.keras.models import Sequential

from tensorflow.keras.layers import Conv2D,
MaxPooling2D, Flatten, Dense, Dropout

from tensorflow.keras.preprocessing.image import
ImageDataGenerator


# Step 1: Load and Preprocess Data
datagen = ImageDataGenerator(rescale=1./255,
validation_split=0.2)


train_generator = datagen.flow_from_directory(
    'dogs_vs_cats',
    target_size=(150, 150),
    batch_size=32,
```

```python
        class_mode='binary',

        subset='training'

)


validation_generator = datagen.flow_from_directory(

    'dogs_vs_cats',

    target_size=(150, 150),

    batch_size=32,

    class_mode='binary',

    subset='validation'

)


# Step 2: Define the CNN Architecture
model = Sequential([

    Conv2D(32, (3, 3), activation='relu', input_shape=(150,
150, 3)),

    MaxPooling2D(pool_size=(2, 2)),


    Conv2D(64, (3, 3), activation='relu'),

    MaxPooling2D(pool_size=(2, 2)),


    Conv2D(128, (3, 3), activation='relu'),
```

```python
    MaxPooling2D(pool_size=(2, 2)),

    Flatten(),
    Dense(128, activation='relu'),
    Dropout(0.5),
    Dense(1, activation='sigmoid')  # Binary classification
])


# Step 3: Compile the Model
model.compile(optimizer='adam',
loss='binary_crossentropy', metrics=['accuracy'])


# Step 4: Train the Model
model.fit(
    train_generator,
    validation_data=validation_generator,
    epochs=10
)


# Step 5: Evaluate the Model
loss, accuracy = model.evaluate(validation_generator)
print(f"Validation Accuracy: {accuracy * 100:.2f}%")
```

Discussion

1. **Model Architecture**:

   o **Input Layer**: Takes in 150x150 RGB images.

   o **Convolutional Layers**: Extract spatial features.

   o **Pooling Layers**: Reduce dimensionality while retaining important features.

   o **Dense Layers**: Perform classification.

2. **Performance**:

   o Test accuracy depends on dataset quality and model complexity.

   o Increasing the number of epochs or layers can improve accuracy but may lead to overfitting.

Comparison: Pre-Trained vs. Custom Models

Feature	Pre-Trained Models	Custom CNN
Ease of Use	Simple to implement	Requires careful design
Accuracy	High for complex datasets	Moderate for simple tasks

Feature	Pre-Trained Models	Custom CNN
Training Time	Faster	Slower
Dataset Requirement	Smaller	Larger

Chapter 8: Advanced Object Detection

Advanced object detection techniques like **YOLO (You Only Look Once)** and face detection using **Haar Cascades** or **DNN-based methods** have transformed computer vision by enabling real-time, highly accurate recognition and classification. This chapter introduces these techniques and provides practical applications, such as pedestrian detection and face recognition.

YOLO (You Only Look Once)

What is YOLO?

YOLO (You Only Look Once) is a real-time object detection system that processes the entire image in one forward pass of a neural network. Unlike traditional methods, YOLO frames object detection as a regression problem, predicting bounding boxes and class probabilities simultaneously.

1. **How YOLO Works:**

- The input image is divided into a grid (e.g., 13x13).

- Each grid cell predicts:

  - Bounding boxes.

  - Confidence scores.

  - Class probabilities.

2. **Advantages**:

   - **Real-time performance**: YOLO can process images at high speeds.

   - **Unified architecture**: A single network performs both localization and classification.

   - **Generalization**: YOLO performs well on diverse datasets.

Real-World Example: Real-Time Pedestrian Detection

Let's use a pre-trained YOLOv3 model to detect pedestrians in a video feed.

Steps:

1. Download the YOLOv3 configuration file, weights, and labels.

2. Load the YOLO model using OpenCV.

3. Process a video stream, draw bounding boxes, and label pedestrians.

Code:

```python
import cv2
import numpy as np

# Step 1: Load YOLO Model
net = cv2.dnn.readNet("yolov3.weights", "yolov3.cfg")
layer_names = net.getLayerNames()
output_layers = [layer_names[i - 1] for i in net.getUnconnectedOutLayers()]

# Load COCO labels
with open("coco.names", "r") as f:
    classes = f.read().strip().split("\n")

# Step 2: Initialize Video Capture
cap = cv2.VideoCapture("pedestrian_video.mp4")

while True:
    ret, frame = cap.read()
    if not ret:
        break
```

```python
    height, width = frame.shape[:2]

    # Step 3: Preprocess Input Image
    blob = cv2.dnn.blobFromImage(frame, 1/255.0, (416,
416), swapRB=True, crop=False)
    net.setInput(blob)

    # Step 4: Run Forward Pass
    outputs = net.forward(output_layers)

    # Step 5: Process Outputs
    for output in outputs:
        for detection in output:
            scores = detection[5:]
            class_id = np.argmax(scores)
            confidence = scores[class_id]

            if confidence > 0.5 and classes[class_id] ==
"person":  # Detect pedestrians
                center_x = int(detection[0] * width)
                center_y = int(detection[1] * height)
                w = int(detection[2] * width)
```

```python
        h = int(detection[3] * height)

        x = int(center_x - w / 2)
        y = int(center_y - h / 2)

        cv2.rectangle(frame, (x, y), (x + w, y + h), (0,
255, 0), 2)
        cv2.putText(frame, "Person", (x, y - 10),
cv2.FONT_HERSHEY_SIMPLEX, 0.5, (0, 255, 0), 2)

    # Step 6: Display Output
    cv2.imshow("Pedestrian Detection", frame)
    if cv2.waitKey(1) & 0xFF == ord("q"):
        break

cap.release()
cv2.destroyAllWindows()
```

Face Detection

Face detection is a specialized object detection task with applications in authentication, surveillance, and augmented reality.

Haar Cascades

Haar Cascades are traditional machine learning-based methods for face detection. They rely on features extracted from image intensities and apply classifiers for detection.

1. **How It Works**:

   o Haar-like features are extracted from the image.

   o An AdaBoost classifier detects faces based on these features.

2. **Advantages**:

   o Lightweight and fast for simple tasks.

   o Does not require large computational resources.

3. **Limitations**:

   o Sensitive to lighting conditions.

   o Struggles with complex poses or occlusions.

Code Example: Detecting Faces with Haar Cascades

python

```
import cv2
```

```
# Load pre-trained Haar Cascade
```

```python
face_cascade =
cv2.CascadeClassifier(cv2.data.haarcascades +
'haarcascade_frontalface_default.xml')


# Load an image

image = cv2.imread('people.jpg')

gray = cv2.cvtColor(image, cv2.COLOR_BGR2GRAY)


# Detect faces

faces = face_cascade.detectMultiScale(gray,
scaleFactor=1.1, minNeighbors=5, minSize=(30, 30))


# Draw bounding boxes around faces

for (x, y, w, h) in faces:

    cv2.rectangle(image, (x, y), (x + w, y + h), (255, 0, 0), 2)


cv2.imshow("Face Detection", image)

cv2.waitKey(0)

cv2.destroyAllWindows()
```

DNN-Based Methods

Deep neural network (DNN)-based methods leverage pre-trained deep learning models for more robust face detection.

1. **Advantages**:
   - Better accuracy with complex poses and lighting.
   - Handles occlusions effectively.

2. **Popular Models**:
   - **OpenCV's DNN Module**: Uses Caffe-based models like ResNet.
   - **MTCNN**: Multi-task CNN for face detection and alignment.

Code Example: Face Detection with OpenCV DNN

python

```
import cv2


# Load pre-trained DNN model
net = cv2.dnn.readNetFromCaffe("deploy.prototxt",
"res10_300x300_ssd_iter_140000.caffemodel")


# Load an image
image = cv2.imread("people.jpg")
(h, w) = image.shape[:2]


# Preprocess the image
```

```python
blob = cv2.dnn.blobFromImage(image, 1.0, (300, 300),
(104.0, 177.0, 123.0))

net.setInput(blob)


# Detect faces

detections = net.forward()


# Draw bounding boxes

for i in range(detections.shape[2]):
    confidence = detections[0, 0, i, 2]
    if confidence > 0.5:
        box = detections[0, 0, i, 3:7] * np.array([w, h, w, h])
        (startX, startY, endX, endY) = box.astype("int")
        cv2.rectangle(image, (startX, startY), (endX, endY),
(0, 255, 0), 2)
        cv2.putText(image, f"{confidence*100:.2f}%",
(startX, startY - 10),
            cv2.FONT_HERSHEY_SIMPLEX, 0.5, (0,
255, 0), 2)


cv2.imshow("Face Detection", image)

cv2.waitKey(0)

cv2.destroyAllWindows()
```

Example: Building a Face Recognition System

A face recognition system involves identifying specific individuals from a face detection task. This typically uses deep learning models like **FaceNet** or **DeepFace** for encoding face embeddings.

Steps:

1. Detect faces in the image.

2. Extract face embeddings using a pre-trained model.

3. Compare embeddings with a database to recognize faces.

Chapter 9: Image Segmentation

Image segmentation is the process of partitioning an image into multiple segments or regions to simplify its analysis. Unlike object detection, which only identifies and localizes objects, segmentation provides detailed boundaries and regions of interest.

Basics of Image Segmentation

Difference Between Detection and Segmentation

Aspect	Object Detection	Image Segmentation
Output	Bounding boxes around objects	Detailed pixel-wise object boundaries
Goal	Identify object classes and locations	Label each pixel with a class
Applications	Pedestrian detection, face recognition	Medical imaging, autonomous driving

Types of Segmentation

1. **Semantic Segmentation**:

   - Labels each pixel with a class but treats all instances of the same class as one.

   - Example: All cars in an image are labeled the same.

2. **Instance Segmentation**:

   - Labels each object instance individually, even if they belong to the same class.

   - Example: Differentiating between two cars in an image.

Segmentation Techniques

Watershed Algorithm

The **watershed algorithm** treats grayscale images as topographic maps, where pixel intensity represents elevation. It segments an image by identifying basins or regions separated by ridges.

1. **How It Works:**

- o   Mark foreground and background regions.

- o   Treat regions as sources of water.

- o   Gradually "flood" the image and separate regions at ridges.

2. **Steps**:

- o   Convert to grayscale and apply thresholding.

- o   Mark regions of interest using distance transform.

- o   Apply the watershed algorithm.

3. **Code Example**:

python

```
import cv2
import numpy as np

# Load image and preprocess
image = cv2.imread('coins.jpg')
gray = cv2.cvtColor(image, cv2.COLOR_BGR2GRAY)
_, binary = cv2.threshold(gray, 0, 255,
cv2.THRESH_BINARY_INV + cv2.THRESH_OTSU)

# Compute distance transform
```

```python
dist_transform = cv2.distanceTransform(binary,
cv2.DIST_L2, 5)

_, markers = cv2.threshold(dist_transform, 0.5 *
dist_transform.max(), 255, 0)


# Marker labeling

markers = np.uint8(markers)

_, labels = cv2.connectedComponents(markers)


# Apply watershed

markers = cv2.watershed(image, markers)

image[markers == -1] = [255, 0, 0]  # Mark boundaries in
red


cv2.imshow('Watershed Segmentation', image)

cv2.waitKey(0)

cv2.destroyAllWindows()
```

GrabCut Algorithm

The **GrabCut algorithm** is an interactive segmentation tool that separates foreground from background using graph cuts.

1. **How It Works**:

- o Initialize a rectangle around the object.

- o Assign labels (foreground, background) iteratively.

- o Use energy minimization to refine segmentation.

2. **Steps**:

- o Load the image and initialize a rectangle.

- o Apply GrabCut using cv2.grabCut().

3. **Code Example**:

python

```python
import cv2
import numpy as np

# Load image
image = cv2.imread('person.jpg')
mask = np.zeros(image.shape[:2], dtype=np.uint8)

# Initialize rectangle for the object
rect = (50, 50, 400, 400)  # x, y, width, height

# Apply GrabCut
```

```python
bg_model = np.zeros((1, 65), dtype=np.float64)  #
Background model

fg_model = np.zeros((1, 65), dtype=np.float64)  #
Foreground model


cv2.grabCut(image, mask, rect, bg_model, fg_model, 5,
cv2.GC_INIT_WITH_RECT)


# Extract the segmented object

mask2 = np.where((mask == 2) | (mask == 0), 0,
1).astype('uint8')

result = image * mask2[:, :, np.newaxis]


cv2.imshow('GrabCut Segmentation', result)

cv2.waitKey(0)

cv2.destroyAllWindows()
```

Deep Learning Approaches

Deep learning has revolutionized image segmentation with models capable of both semantic and instance segmentation.

U-Net

U-Net is a convolutional network architecture designed for biomedical image segmentation. Its U-shaped structure enables both feature extraction and localization.

1. **How U-Net Works**:

   o Encoder: Downsamples the image, extracting features.

   o Decoder: Upsamples the feature maps, generating a segmented output.

2. **Applications**:

   o Medical imaging (e.g., tumor segmentation).

   o Satellite imagery.

3. **Code Example**:

python

```
import tensorflow as tf
from tensorflow.keras.layers import Input, Conv2D, MaxPooling2D, UpSampling2D, concatenate


# Define U-Net architecture
inputs = Input((128, 128, 1))


# Encoder
conv1 = Conv2D(64, (3, 3), activation='relu', padding='same')(inputs)
```

```python
pool1 = MaxPooling2D((2, 2))(conv1)


conv2 = Conv2D(128, (3, 3), activation='relu',
padding='same')(pool1)
pool2 = MaxPooling2D((2, 2))(conv2)


# Decoder
up1 = UpSampling2D((2, 2))(pool2)
concat1 = concatenate([conv2, up1])
conv3 = Conv2D(64, (3, 3), activation='relu',
padding='same')(concat1)


up2 = UpSampling2D((2, 2))(conv3)
concat2 = concatenate([conv1, up2])
outputs = Conv2D(1, (1, 1), activation='sigmoid')(concat2)


model = tf.keras.models.Model(inputs, outputs)
model.compile(optimizer='adam',
loss='binary_crossentropy', metrics=['accuracy'])
```

Mask R-CNN

Mask R-CNN is an instance segmentation framework that extends Faster R-CNN by predicting pixel-level masks for each object.

1. **How Mask R-CNN Works**:

   o **Region Proposal Network (RPN)**:
      Identifies object regions.

   o **Classification and Bounding Box
      Regression**: Classifies and refines regions.

   o **Mask Head**: Generates segmentation masks
      for each object.

2. **Applications**:

   o Autonomous driving (e.g., lane and object
      detection).

   o Augmented reality.

3. **Code Example**:

python

```python
import cv2
from mrcnn import model as modellib
from mrcnn.config import Config

# Define Mask R-CNN Config
class InferenceConfig(Config):
    NAME = "object"
    NUM_CLASSES = 1 + 80  # COCO dataset (80 classes)
    GPU_COUNT = 1
```

```python
IMAGES_PER_GPU = 1

config = InferenceConfig()

# Load Pre-trained Model
model = modellib.MaskRCNN(mode="inference",
config=config, model_dir="logs")

model.load_weights("mask_rcnn_coco.h5",
by_name=True)

# Load Image
image = cv2.imread("example.jpg")
results = model.detect([image], verbose=1)

# Visualize Results
r = results[0]
model.display_instances(image, r['rois'], r['masks'],
r['class_ids'], r['scores'])
```

Chapter 10: Building Real-World Applications

In this chapter, we'll bring together the skills you've developed to build two practical computer vision projects: **Traffic Sign Recognition** and a **Virtual Makeup Application**. These projects demonstrate how image processing, machine learning, and deep learning concepts are applied end-to-end, from data preparation to deployment.

End-to-End Project 1: Traffic Sign Recognition

Traffic sign recognition is a critical task in autonomous vehicles, enabling them to detect and classify road signs. In this project, you'll build a system to recognize traffic signs using a convolutional neural network (CNN).

Step 1: Dataset Preparation and Augmentation

1. **Dataset**:

- Use a dataset like the German Traffic Sign Recognition Benchmark (GTSRB), which contains images of various traffic signs.

2. **Loading the Dataset**:

- Organize the dataset into folders for each traffic sign class.

- Split the dataset into training, validation, and testing sets.

3. **Data Augmentation**:

- Apply transformations to increase data diversity, such as rotation, flipping, and brightness adjustment.

4. **Code for Data Loading and Augmentation**:

python

```
from tensorflow.keras.preprocessing.image import
ImageDataGenerator

# Set up data directories
train_dir = "data/train"
val_dir = "data/validation"

# Data augmentation for training
train_datagen = ImageDataGenerator(
```

```python
    rescale=1.0/255,
    rotation_range=15,
    width_shift_range=0.1,
    height_shift_range=0.1,
    zoom_range=0.2,
    horizontal_flip=False
)


val_datagen = ImageDataGenerator(rescale=1.0/255)


train_generator = train_datagen.flow_from_directory(
    train_dir,
    target_size=(64, 64),
    batch_size=32,
    class_mode='categorical'
)


val_generator = val_datagen.flow_from_directory(
    val_dir,
    target_size=(64, 64),
    batch_size=32,
    class_mode='categorical'
```

)

Step 2: Model Training

1. **Define the CNN**:

   o Build a CNN to classify traffic signs into their respective categories.

2. **Compile and Train**:

   o Use categorical crossentropy as the loss function and an optimizer like Adam.

3. **Code for Training the Model**:

python

```python
from tensorflow.keras.models import Sequential

from tensorflow.keras.layers import Conv2D, MaxPooling2D, Flatten, Dense, Dropout


# Define the CNN model
model = Sequential([

    Conv2D(32, (3, 3), activation='relu', input_shape=(64, 64, 3)),

    MaxPooling2D(pool_size=(2, 2)),

    Conv2D(64, (3, 3), activation='relu'),

    MaxPooling2D(pool_size=(2, 2)),
```

```python
    Flatten(),

    Dense(128, activation='relu'),

    Dropout(0.5),

    Dense(43, activation='softmax')  # Assuming 43 traffic
sign classes

])


# Compile the model

model.compile(optimizer='adam',
loss='categorical_crossentropy', metrics=['accuracy'])


# Train the model

model.fit(train_generator, validation_data=val_generator,
epochs=10)
```

Step 3: Deployment

1. **Save the Model**:

python


```python
model.save("traffic_sign_model.h5")
```

2. **Real-Time Inference**:

- o Load the model and classify signs from live video feeds.

python

```python
import cv2
from tensorflow.keras.models import load_model
import numpy as np

# Load the trained model
model = load_model("traffic_sign_model.h5")

# Real-time video feed
cap = cv2.VideoCapture(0)
while True:
    ret, frame = cap.read()
    if not ret:
        break

    # Preprocess the frame
    resized = cv2.resize(frame, (64, 64))
    input_data = np.expand_dims(resized / 255.0, axis=0)
```

```
# Predict the class

predictions = model.predict(input_data)

class_id = np.argmax(predictions)

confidence = np.max(predictions)


# Display the result

cv2.putText(frame, f"Sign: {class_id}, Confidence:
{confidence:.2f}",

        (10, 30), cv2.FONT_HERSHEY_SIMPLEX, 1,
(0, 255, 0), 2)

cv2.imshow("Traffic Sign Recognition", frame)


if cv2.waitKey(1) & 0xFF == ord("q"):

    break


cap.release()

cv2.destroyAllWindows()
```

End-to-End Project 2: Virtual Makeup Application

A virtual makeup application overlays cosmetic effects, like lipstick or blush, onto a user's face. This involves detecting facial landmarks and applying transformations to specific regions.

Step 1: Using Facial Landmarks

Facial landmarks identify key points on a face, such as eyes, nose, and lips. Dlib and OpenCV can be used to extract these landmarks.

1. **Detect Landmarks**:
   - o Use a pre-trained model for facial landmark detection.
2. **Code for Landmark Detection**:

python

```
import cv2
import dlib


# Load pre-trained facial landmark detector
detector = dlib.get_frontal_face_detector()
predictor =
dlib.shape_predictor("shape_predictor_68_face_landmarks.
dat")


# Load the image
image = cv2.imread("face.jpg")
```

```python
gray = cv2.cvtColor(image, cv2.COLOR_BGR2GRAY)

# Detect faces
faces = detector(gray)
for face in faces:
    landmarks = predictor(gray, face)

    # Draw landmarks
    for n in range(68):  # 68 landmarks
        x = landmarks.part(n).x
        y = landmarks.part(n).y
        cv2.circle(image, (x, y), 2, (0, 255, 0), -1)

cv2.imshow("Facial Landmarks", image)
cv2.waitKey(0)
cv2.destroyAllWindows()
```

Step 2: Overlay Makeup

1. **Define Makeup Regions**:
   o Identify regions for lipstick (lips) or blush (cheeks) using landmarks.

2. **Apply Effects**:

- o Use image masking to overlay color or patterns.

3. **Code for Lipstick Application**:

python

```
import numpy as np


# Extract lip landmarks
lip_points = np.array([(landmarks.part(i).x,
landmarks.part(i).y) for i in range(48, 61)])


# Create a mask for lips
mask = np.zeros_like(image)
cv2.fillPoly(mask, [lip_points], (0, 0, 255))  # Red lipstick


# Blend the mask with the original image
result = cv2.addWeighted(image, 1, mask, 0.4, 0)


cv2.imshow("Virtual Makeup - Lipstick", result)
cv2.waitKey(0)
cv2.destroyAllWindows()
```

Step 3: Enhance Realism

1. **Blur and Feathering**:

    o Apply Gaussian blur to smooth the makeup
       edges.

2. **Dynamic Adjustment**:

    o Adjust opacity based on lighting conditions
       or user preferences.

Chapter 11: Deployment and Scalability

Deploying computer vision models in production requires careful consideration of scalability, latency, and integration. This chapter covers how to deploy models using Flask or Django for API-based services and optimize them for real-time applications using techniques like model quantization and TensorRT.

Deploying Models

Saving and Loading Models

Saving trained models ensures they can be reused or shared without retraining, while loading allows integration into real-world applications.

1. **Saving a Model**:

   o   Save a trained model in TensorFlow or PyTorch.

   o   Example (TensorFlow/Keras):

python

```
# Save model in HDF5 format
model.save("model.h5")
```

- o Example (PyTorch):

python

```
import torch
# Save model state dictionary
torch.save(model.state_dict(), "model.pth")
```

2. **Loading a Model**:
   - o Reload the saved model for inference.
   - o Example (TensorFlow/Keras):

python

```
from tensorflow.keras.models import load_model
model = load_model("model.h5")
```

- o Example (PyTorch):

python

```
model.load_state_dict(torch.load("model.pth"))
model.eval()  # Set model to evaluation mode
```

Using Flask/Django for APIs

Flask and Django are Python frameworks that allow you to serve models as APIs for integration with web and mobile applications.

Using Flask

1. **Set Up Flask**:

   o Install Flask: pip install flask.

2. **Create an API Endpoint**:

   o Example:

python

```
from flask import Flask, request, jsonify

import tensorflow as tf

import numpy as np

import cv2


app = Flask(__name__)


# Load the model
model = tf.keras.models.load_model("model.h5")
```

```python
@app.route("/predict", methods=["POST"])
def predict():
    file = request.files['image']
    image = cv2.imdecode(np.frombuffer(file.read(),
np.uint8), cv2.IMREAD_COLOR)
    image_resized = cv2.resize(image, (64, 64)) / 255.0
    image_resized = np.expand_dims(image_resized,
axis=0)

    predictions = model.predict(image_resized)
    result = np.argmax(predictions)

    return jsonify({"class_id": int(result), "confidence":
float(predictions[0][result])})

if __name__ == "__main__":
    app.run(debug=True)
```

3. **Test the API**:

   o Use tools like Postman or CURL to test the
      /predict endpoint.

Using Django

1. **Set Up Django**:
   o Install Django: pip install django.
2. **Create a View for Predictions**:
   o Example:

python

```python
from django.http import JsonResponse
import tensorflow as tf
import numpy as np
import cv2

model = tf.keras.models.load_model("model.h5")

def predict_view(request):
    file = request.FILES['image']
    image = cv2.imdecode(np.frombuffer(file.read(),
np.uint8), cv2.IMREAD_COLOR)
    image_resized = cv2.resize(image, (64, 64)) / 255.0
    image_resized = np.expand_dims(image_resized,
axis=0)

    predictions = model.predict(image_resized)
    result = np.argmax(predictions)
```

```python
    return JsonResponse({"class_id": int(result),
"confidence": float(predictions[0][result])})
```

Optimizing for Real-Time Applications

Deploying models in real-time scenarios, like video
analytics or IoT devices, requires optimization to minimize
latency and resource usage.

Model Quantization

Model quantization reduces model size and computational
cost by converting floating-point weights (e.g., FP32) to
lower precision (e.g., INT8).

1. **Advantages**:

   o   Faster inference.

   o   Reduced memory usage.

2. **Quantization with TensorFlow Lite**:

python

import tensorflow as tf

Convert model to TensorFlow Lite with quantization

```python
converter = tf.lite.TFLiteConverter.from_keras_model(model)
converter.optimizations = [tf.lite.Optimize.DEFAULT]
tflite_model = converter.convert()

# Save the quantized model
with open("model_quantized.tflite", "wb") as f:
    f.write(tflite_model)
```

3. **Running the Quantized Model**:
   - Use TensorFlow Lite Interpreter for inference.

python

```python
import tflite_runtime.interpreter as tflite

interpreter = tflite.Interpreter(model_path="model_quantized.tflite")
interpreter.allocate_tensors()

input_details = interpreter.get_input_details()
output_details = interpreter.get_output_details()

# Prepare input
```

```python
input_data = np.expand_dims(image,
axis=0).astype(np.float32)

interpreter.set_tensor(input_details[0]['index'], input_data)


interpreter.invoke()

output = interpreter.get_tensor(output_details[0]['index'])
```

Acceleration with TensorRT

TensorRT is NVIDIA's platform for optimizing deep learning models for GPUs. It accelerates inference by applying optimizations like kernel fusion and precision tuning.

1. **Converting Models to TensorRT**:

   o Export your model to ONNX format.

python

```python
import torch


# Export PyTorch model to ONNX
torch.onnx.export(model, dummy_input, "model.onnx")
```

   o Use TensorRT to convert the ONNX model.

bash

```
trtexec --onnx=model.onnx --saveEngine=model.trt --fp16
```

2. **Running TensorRT Models**:

   o Use the TensorRT engine for real-time inference on NVIDIA GPUs.

```
python
```

```
import tensorrt as trt
```

Scaling Up

1. **Horizontal Scaling**:

   o Deploy the model on multiple servers and distribute traffic using load balancers.

2. **Edge Deployment**:

   o Deploy optimized models on edge devices (e.g., Jetson Nano, Raspberry Pi).

3. **Cloud Integration**:

   o Use services like AWS SageMaker, Google AI Platform, or Azure Machine Learning for scalable deployment.

Chapter 12: Future Directions in Computer Vision

Computer vision is evolving rapidly, with advancements transforming industries like healthcare, transportation, and entertainment. In this chapter, we'll explore current trends, challenges, and how you can stay updated in this dynamic field.

Trends and Challenges

1. Explainability in AI

As computer vision systems become integral to critical applications, such as autonomous vehicles and healthcare diagnostics, the need for explainability—understanding how AI makes decisions—has grown.

1. **What is Explainability?**

    o Explainability involves making the predictions of AI models interpretable to humans.

- For example, understanding why a vision model flagged a tumor as malignant.

2. **Why It Matters**:

   - **Trust**: Users and stakeholders are more likely to trust transparent systems.

   - **Debugging**: Helps identify biases and errors in models.

   - **Compliance**: Legal frameworks like GDPR demand AI transparency.

3. **Techniques for Explainability**:

   - **Saliency Maps**:

     - Highlights regions of an image that influence the model's predictions.

     - Example:

python

```
import tensorflow as tf
import matplotlib.pyplot as plt


# Compute gradient of class output w.r.t input image
with tf.GradientTape() as tape:
    tape.watch(input_image)
    predictions = model(input_image)
    loss = predictions[:, target_class_index]
```

```
gradients = tape.gradient(loss, input_image)

plt.imshow(gradients[0].numpy())
```

- **SHAP and LIME**:
  - Frameworks for explaining predictions through local approximations.

---

2. Ethical Considerations

The increasing use of computer vision raises ethical concerns that must be addressed to ensure responsible deployment.

1. **Bias in Models**:
   - Models may exhibit biases in object detection or facial recognition due to skewed training datasets.
   - Example: Facial recognition systems often struggle with accuracy for underrepresented demographics.
   - **Solution**: Diversify datasets and apply fairness-aware algorithms.

2. **Privacy Issues**:

- Surveillance systems using facial recognition can infringe on privacy.

- **Solution**: Anonymization techniques like pixelation or blurring.

3. **Deepfakes**:

- Manipulating images or videos to create convincing fake content.

- **Solution**: Deepfake detection algorithms leveraging AI to identify tampered media.

4. **Autonomous Systems**:

- Ethical dilemmas arise in scenarios like self-driving cars prioritizing human lives.

- **Solution**: Develop guidelines to standardize decision-making processes in AI-driven systems.

\

How to Stay Updated

The fast pace of innovation in computer vision demands continuous learning. Here's how you can stay ahead.

1. Online Resources

1. **Courses**:

   o **Deep Learning Specialization by Andrew Ng** (Coursera):

   - Covers foundational and advanced deep learning concepts.

   o **CS231n: Convolutional Neural Networks for Visual Recognition** (Stanford):

   - A detailed course on computer vision and deep learning.

2. **Websites**:

   o **Papers with Code**:

   - Explore state-of-the-art models with links to research papers and implementations.

   o **Kaggle**:

   - Practice on computer vision datasets and participate in competitions.

2. Forums and Communities

1. **GitHub**:

   o Follow repositories for cutting-edge tools like OpenCV, TensorFlow, and PyTorch.

- Explore open-source projects to understand practical applications.

2. **Reddit**:
   - Subreddits like r/MachineLearning and r/computervision are great for discussions and resources.

3. **Stack Overflow**:
   - Engage with the community to solve coding challenges and share insights.

---

3. Conferences and Workshops

1. **Conferences**:
   - **CVPR (Computer Vision and Pattern Recognition)**:
     - Premier venue for showcasing breakthroughs in computer vision.
   - **ICCV (International Conference on Computer Vision)**:
     - Covers theoretical and applied advancements.
   - **ECCV (European Conference on Computer Vision)**:
     - Focuses on state-of-the-art research in Europe.

2. **Workshops**:

- o Attending workshops helps gain hands-on experience and network with experts.

---

4. Tools and Platforms

1. **Google Colab**:

    - o Free cloud-based platform for training and deploying models.

2. **Hugging Face**:

    - o Access pre-trained models and tools for computer vision and NLP.

3. **PyImageSearch**:

    - o Tutorials and guides for practical computer vision tasks.

Emerging Trends in Computer Vision

1. **3D Vision and AR/VR**:

    - o Techniques like depth estimation and scene reconstruction are enabling immersive experiences in augmented and virtual reality.

2. **Generative Models**:

- GANs (Generative Adversarial Networks) are being used to create realistic images, super-resolution, and synthetic data.

3. **Edge AI**:

- Deploying computer vision models on edge devices (e.g., smartphones, drones) for real-time processing with minimal latency.

4. **Federated Learning**:

- Collaborative training across decentralized devices to improve model performance without compromising privacy.

Conclusion

The journey through the world of computer vision has been a transformative one, exploring its fundamentals, applications, and advanced techniques. As we conclude this book, let's reflect on the key learnings, challenges, and opportunities that lie ahead in the ever-evolving field of computer vision.

Key Takeaways

1. The Foundations of Computer Vision

We began with the basics of digital images, learning how computers perceive them as numerical data—pixels, channels, and resolutions. These concepts provided a foundation for understanding image processing techniques such as filtering, transformations, and histogram equalization. With tools like OpenCV, we saw how these techniques are applied to enhance image quality and extract valuable features.

2. Object Detection and Tracking

Object detection is a cornerstone of computer vision, with applications ranging from surveillance to autonomous vehicles. Techniques like contour detection and tracking algorithms such as MeanShift and CamShift introduced us to the art of identifying and following objects in dynamic environments. These classical methods laid the groundwork for more advanced deep learning-based approaches.

3. Deep Learning Revolution

The advent of deep learning has marked a turning point for computer vision. Convolutional Neural Networks (CNNs) have unlocked the potential to automate feature extraction and learn hierarchical patterns, outperforming traditional methods. Pre-trained models like MobileNet and ResNet, along with architectures like U-Net and Mask R-CNN, demonstrated the power of transfer learning and advanced segmentation.

4. Practical Applications

Through real-world projects, we bridged the gap between theory and practice:

- **Traffic Sign Recognition**: Showed how CNNs and dataset augmentation enable robust classification systems for autonomous driving.

- **Virtual Makeup Application**: Highlighted the creative applications of facial landmark detection in augmented reality.

These projects illustrated how to combine algorithms, frameworks, and tools into deployable systems.

5. Deployment and Scalability

Bringing computer vision models to production is a critical step. By learning to deploy models via APIs using Flask or

Django, and optimizing them with techniques like quantization and TensorRT, we explored how to scale vision solutions for real-time and resource-constrained environments.

6. Challenges and the Future

The challenges of explainability, ethical concerns, and privacy in AI were examined. These considerations are critical as computer vision systems become increasingly integrated into our lives. Meanwhile, emerging trends like AR/VR, generative models, and edge computing are shaping the future, offering exciting new frontiers to explore.

Real-World Impact

Computer vision is no longer confined to research labs—it is transforming industries and solving real-world problems. Here are some examples of its profound impact:

1. **Healthcare**:
    - Computer vision enables early diagnosis of diseases through medical imaging, improving outcomes and saving lives.
    - Projects like tumor segmentation and disease detection showcase the life-saving potential of vision technologies.

2. **Autonomous Systems**:

- Self-driving cars and drones rely on computer vision to navigate and interact with their surroundings, promising safer and more efficient transportation.

3. **Retail and E-commerce**:

- Visual search and product recommendation systems are enhancing customer experiences and driving sales.

4. **Environment and Agriculture**:

- Monitoring wildlife, analyzing crop health, and detecting pollution are some of the ways computer vision is aiding sustainability efforts.

These applications emphasize that computer vision is not just a technical pursuit—it is a force for societal and environmental progress.

Embracing the Challenges

While the potential of computer vision is vast, challenges remain. Here's how we can address them:

1. **Bias and Fairness**:

- Diverse datasets and fairness-aware algorithms are essential to prevent discriminatory outcomes.

2. **Explainability and Trust**:

- Tools like saliency maps and interpretable models can help users understand AI decisions, fostering trust and transparency.

3. **Privacy and Ethics**:

   - Implementing privacy-preserving techniques like anonymization and federated learning ensures responsible deployment.

4. **Accessibility**:

   - Simplifying tools and democratizing access to resources can empower more individuals to contribute to the field.

By tackling these challenges head-on, we can build a future where computer vision benefits everyone.

Your Role in Shaping the Future

The field of computer vision is dynamic and ever-changing, with opportunities for growth and innovation. Here's how you can make an impact:

1. **Continuous Learning**:

   - Stay updated with the latest research and tools through platforms like Papers with Code, GitHub, and conferences like CVPR and ICCV.

2. **Experimentation**:

- Apply what you've learned in this book to new projects. Whether it's building applications or contributing to open-source repositories, practical experience is invaluable.

3. **Collaboration**:

   - Join communities on Reddit, Stack Overflow, and Kaggle to exchange ideas and solve challenges together.

4. **Ethical Stewardship**:

   - Advocate for responsible AI practices and contribute to projects that prioritize fairness, inclusivity, and societal good.

Looking Ahead

The next decade promises to redefine computer vision. Emerging trends include:

1. **3D Vision**:

   - Advances in depth estimation and point cloud analysis are opening new possibilities for robotics and AR/VR.

2. **Generative AI**:

   - Models like GANs are not only creating realistic images but also revolutionizing industries like fashion and gaming.

3. **Edge Computing**:

   o The ability to deploy vision models on low-power devices like smartphones and IoT sensors is driving real-time applications.

4. **Cross-Disciplinary Integration**:

   o Combining computer vision with fields like natural language processing and reinforcement learning is unlocking new capabilities.

The convergence of these trends will shape the next wave of innovation, offering limitless possibilities for those ready to explore them.

Final Words

Computer vision is a field of creativity, discovery, and impact. From enhancing healthcare to powering the vehicles of the future, it has the potential to transform our world in profound ways. This book has provided you with the tools, techniques, and insights to embark on your journey in this exciting domain.

Remember, the key to success lies in curiosity, perseverance, and a commitment to learning. Whether you're solving pressing problems or building the next big innovation, you are now equipped to make a meaningful contribution to the field.

The journey doesn't end here—it begins. Step into the world of computer vision and shape the future.

Happy coding, and may your vision projects always succeed!

Acknowledgments: Thank you for reading and being part of this exploration into computer vision. The possibilities are infinite, and the next breakthroughs might just come from your work.